www.finishinglinepress.com

CATCH A GLOW

poems by

Karl Michael Iglesias

Finishing Line Press
Georgetown, Kentucky

CATCH A GLOW

For Mami

ACKNOWLEDGMENTS

The following publications have supported my work and have previously
given earlier versions of these poems a home:

*Apogee, The Acentos Review, The Breakwater Review, The Florida Review,
Rhino Poetry, Kweli Journal.*

PRAISE DANCE AT UTUADO and TONIGHT'S BLACKOUT appear in
Breakbeat Poets Vol. 4: LatiNext (Haymarket Books, 2020)

Publisher: Leah Huete de Maines
Editor: Christen Kincaid
Cover Art and Design: Christian Martir
Author Photo: JBIH Photography

Order online: www.finishinglinepress.com
        also available on amazon.com

Author inquiries and mail orders:
Finishing Line Press
PO Box 1626
Georgetown, Kentucky 40324
USA

Table of Contents

invisible ink, I had to read things that wasn't there
—Jay-Z

from under the water then there's fresh air
—Lil Wayne

SIGHTING

On September 20th, at approximately 615 AM AST Maria made landfall in Yabucoa, Puerto Rico as a strong category 4 hurricane with maximum sustained winds of 155 mph.

hot breath heaving   or uproot   steam burn   twigs turn dart
same speed   the aim   and fire-sprint
as god   it is   name-say i pine
my hommage   and also   what details my push
first it was play
but waves grew with my fervor
ask the grumpy coral   i am weightless boulder   but wrecking sneeze-swift
my eye is for intake   i gather in the blood   kept turning on key
saw a village of frogs ascend   and divide
saw diaspora   placed them in rain stick   earth ear-hustling am i plague

                              that depends
                              on who dies
                              in the summoning

on the timing of clouds   under the veil of prophecy   cover
your home   then mourn the tostones in the walls
brimstone for bash   in the whistle
of this traveling church   to the lighthouse   for staying
that empty   to the desperate
beach greeting me   taking nothing   empty palm   trees dress
path floral for my retreat   getting close   relish the testament
doubt in pruned hands   constant   praying around my gaze   in satellite
farms made ritual   and scattered   seafoam ash
abuelos sin nietos   hallway light left on

                              and of course
                              Juracán was the name that
                              belted

"sensacional cuando salió en la madrugada"

RECEIVED NEW

After Frank O'Hara

rippling pond of bustelo   coffee timer beeps from kitchen   steam settles
his roommate   goes to work and the sun drags him out of bed   glow of his
lamp   still on from last night   he exhales a prayer   hoping he charged
his phone before he fell asleep   to the news   burning cool moonlight
midnight fireplace sleep mode   will shut off   eventually   if idle avoiding
the dark   his coffee   light   half a spoon of sugar   gets to use his electric
toothbrush today   for the first time   after it charges   phone is on ten
percent   battery saver mode   emails glued to his skin   thumbs through
check online correspondence   message   from his roommate   divides
bills   consolidated edison   national grid   optimum   internet   paid
attention   message   he learns how

angry miriam was at her husband's sleep apnea machine   for needing so
much from her   in maunabo   natalio stopped breathing   in the middle
of the night   now everyone is shaking   on the floor   couldn't do nothing
braulio died from a heart attack in the parking lot of his clinic   waiting for it
to open used to be 24 hours   carmen's oxygen machine shut off   last
week   he gasps   or hears one

OPEN FOR BUSINESS

timbales calling   from the lobby at the san juan marriott   resort & casino

   which was finally packed   with fanning tourists   and not just emergency

workers   checking in   air conditioned   skin peeling   savior spends   on sights

   mountain communities   are still desperate   for power   supplies   damaged

resorts   attention   hotels are back up and running   industry is critical

   long-term recovery here   *it's like the storm came through yesterday*

said the mountains of yabucoa   along with their children   been relying

on a generator   to survive we need help   another night

in limbo   spent on the porch   in the dark

OFRENDA

joselito has a generator that his son sent him
from florida   he has been using it to power the flood
light   down the road   every evening   since dia de los reyes
offering our bario a makeshift lamp post   cayey's north star   i take

a little shine from our neo-moon to inspect how my calloused fingers
translate chords   my hamaca offers
the usual waltz   I offer pitorro de quenepa
to evelyn and her husband next door

but they never except   she offers una tasita tivia
and how could i say no   i offer my cuatro   cup of humming
sugar   my quickened bones croon a bolero out   the night
is warm brick of chocolate surrendering to simmered milk

sweet blood   i offer tune to relentless mosquitos   baiting
the bats   they offer salsa   offer clashing shadows and their best
smile   swift wings   a striking turn of page   i can barely read the
notes off my crinkled hymnal but if i angle it just right   i can

catch a glow over my shoulder and i play on   coquis
whistle by the thousands   offer to fill the air with a call and
response   a coro-pregón of burning candles
on porches   listening   constantly   joselito keens that

his son is not
coming back but should
hear from him
soon

TONIGHT'S BLACKOUT

fault on transmission line   the grid dropped
and eventually outage   the deep sigh of dimming lights
all long-blink   for the outrage   of an endless 48 hours

got pressed   with flat lines   distressed temples
bent brows   based off the uncertainty
based off the constant jettison

the coconut gets more light than luis   and at dawn
i fell asleep at the gas station and i'm told there is   enough
but we stay waiting   this year has been unplugged respiration

i need breath   and un pastelón calientito
and representation in the senate   this is big stick   mi pana speak softly
save your voice   they take it   in rhythm   the way nurse treats pulse

WHEN SOMEONE ASKS ME IF MY FAMILY HAS POWER IN PUERTO RICO

it is usually with a lilied exhale   drained
from a distant church pew
the name of my tired island
offered as off-white pall
stitched of condolence   circle of pale seagulls
but i am not sure who has died
and who has electricity or
how long my cousin gordo will be
stuck at the airport   stalled and
disconnected   tethered nets gathering flotsam

if something was wrong   i'd know
right ?

submerged staggering undercurrent
ear squelching ground

SHUTTERED NEW

education   announced   closure
schools   erased in endless   summer
taking into account
sharp drop   in enrollment
amid island   economic   slump
families departure
and american desks   today: english only
first winter   coat   new york radiator hiss
tropic piping haunting
fever   that opens   windows in january

in the coming weeks
ms torres to lose   her job
joined strike   in the mayhem
after the police   fired tear gas and pepper
spray to end   gathered to oppose
decimate what remained   more to leave
we're overwhelmed,   said the need to express our indignation
                            people
who are suffering
marched down gold mile   heart of the financial district
bank buildings   glass high-rises
they won't stop us,   salsa blared
scuffle in riot gear   before a drizzle
briefly dampened   wooden shields
dressed in charcoal   covering faces with bandanas   tear gas
chaos has been arrested   and injured
covering   windows with plywood
and hurricane shutters   standoff with police   who fired
downward   spiral wrath   judge handling
the island's bankruptcy   an entity not elected by the people

we found out   *from the press*

8

NEWBORN DECLARES INDEPENDENCE INSIDE VIEQUES HOSPITAL

Hurricane Maria closes Vieques' only labor and delivery room.

and deliver me again
burst me into
your occasional rooster
a paranda through the ribs
do not hold me

who rocks the arch
of my crib
is my god   and you took
my mama
because you couldn't deliver

her son   and now I   godless
    baby-howl   pitter pat

    finger paint
         on the walls

             of congress

MOVING OUT

my spine spoils
into an open cardboard box
headlining a summer yard sale

a buzzing chest stuffed with fading power
rangers, monsters and mutants,

       a bundle of boy
       sold for the low

JIBARO

i
showered
with   warm
water   heated
by   fire
furnace   broken
bathing
with
plastic bucket
and cup
washcloth
baptism scrubbing dead
skin of sand devoid of sun
shivering in a tub
touched by winter i am
closer to an island i have
only been to once   my mother
in the distance urging me to listen
to the clicking of copper colored
frogs and chickens sifting through
feed   i could hear it too   just
beyond 28th and brown
and the hills of snow
that separate the
streets from the
sidewalk

"a medio día ya noticia confirmada"

LEFT THE HOTEL THAT FEMA STOPPED PAYING FOR ON FRIDAY

ended up at a shelter   after-action   making the president
look bad   hibiscus yawns
on a once-road
baked in clay   cabo rojo to brooklyn
trickle of feet

is dew drip   this is the first morning
of homelessness   making the president look
bad   my families everywhere   you see
thaliana and her son facetiming tio cruz on the curb
sol   our grand marshall

cries in spanish   in the wake   making the president look bad   in a
warning
by the unsung   agency in the parade
in a hotel lobby   by the airport
there is nowhere to warm   churn a family-laugh
there ain't goodwill   for evicted psalms   pinned

making the president   look
bad   blue birds saying everything   they heard from
someone else   the rent late
displaced on the balls of feet   trauma for thunder
bruno lying on asphalt   emergency lane

and we worry for the length of   rest in a blanket of sirens
and the atlantic ocean   ruins
and they build their beacon   and cause the brick
tower to deteriorate   and they lit a donation   and welcomed
the street light   and ain't it hard just to live?

BATTERED NEW

maria pleads
six months for help
looking after maria
transplanted struggle
to put down   roots in central
we are forgotten

people   it's been almost
six months since maria
lures   spring
to fund comeback
break maria
some good news

maria still pleading for help
six months
made maria victim
citizens   yet not
american more
isolated maria   won't leave for main

land note   onboarding
maria lingers into a disaster
like an afterthought
maria hits
demands history
division of sending

award maria
help in aims
inspire bow & arrow
attract council
power slowly
maria is better to roots

water return
300 dogs following maria
rescued from celebration exodus
maria nearly grows as island
struggles to rebound from maria
can't keep lights on

blows out
first seed to ever
settle maria
why maker
does restoring full
power seem like a never-ending

task   skipped white
house still needs Maria
to visit   aid   relief
for maria   unions clash
over proposed players
maria never before madness

after insane
seeded upset
we just believed
in each other
why shocking   maria is better
will stand alone as gold

stunning recipe for maria
will change   what is
in maria   we are real
for one   still dying
staying maria   victory
validation effect

benefit from
a historic upset
art museums review maria
face recovery
locker after   close
maria moves upset

post-storm chaos
face future uncertain
welcomes seed upset
club faces   defeat
react upset
reunited   maria flees

HALF OF THE PARROTS DISAPPEARED

near the south's end
of the viaduct
the tropical forest
I stand with the pummeled mountain
of two dozen kids from the neighborhood
a couple of turquoise tipped wings
sunshine from crashing
passion fruit   without canopy
I want laws that shake
hands   I am of the shaken
the ones who recover through gardening
camouflage   a fledgling coalition
of churches   headquartered at the end
I go in more

resistant to hurricanes
and I only face
hurricanes   topple the nest
after I break
through the shell my vital recovery
for the species   we handful the dirt
get another flock reintroduced wild
I boycotted grapes   up when the march cut
through 6th street
now return with south side
english   cause you can't turn
the deez, doze, dat off
or not want to send all the money you make
back to your family

EVAPORATING

my feet submerge first
tide soaking a heap of dirty laundry
a family of empty outfits floating
knee level

                    hollow clothes

        spent swimmers

                                        vanishing bodies
            i, in wilderness, am

                         dead all around me

"y en la tarde materia olvidada"

BAYAMANACO AT THE CREMATORIUM

"3000 people did not die in the two hurricanes that hit Puerto Rico"
—Donald Trump

i was asked not to count the names etched in ash
it is uncertain which dried mounds have drowned

or which dry mouths have burned
so we do not count the dead

after juracán roared
department of public safety

reported deaths   have been engulfing
in stars   old man fire   algid hallways lit by taíno

torch   most of this place is a melting candle
powerless   night is a blanket of sweat   fatigue

i have seen these same solemn ashes spread
across campos and the crystal shallows of culebra

i gather them now   names deserving of echoes   a lit
furnace   oven of russet hearts   asthma   dehydration

all glowing in a halo of rainwater
thin bones speak firewood

cracking   quick retort of desiccated
branches hacked from where they burgeon

after the sky of aguada
rushed   children into the surf

and the sea deluged to meet the storm
over   bodies have been cremated

and to think   i thought that there would be nothing
left to burn

COVERED NEW

"At MDC Guaynabo prison, approximately 120 inmates were kept locked in their cell for nearly seven days following the storm."

seven by ten cell is sentencing policy

                    stench of seven-day unflushed toilet

i am the third inmate   sleeping on the floor

bond in perpetual danger now   marshaled with flood zone

panic to the lockdown

             had no idea where the water was coming from

broken glass needs redemption   the guard's eyes maybe-kill

zip tie intimate like inmate   sobbed in rags for so much   blood

design this sentence   gather like buckets   flush

facedown in goldenrod   pepper sprayed   the rinse

serving an eternity   dipped left cheek   pursed lips

faced with cellmate   tear-swell through the squint

dropper to feed the planted   city dew leaking from the ceiling

wrist to lavender we are bleeding on the inside   release

bullet the bruising   may our families know   we are alive

PRAISE DANCE AT UTUADO

i was last found
joy-tumbling in a ring of stones
to three trombones
harmony

of stabs
i am pierced   sheet music
under vanishing amber
leering upward

pleading a fall
to pour out
tributary of picked scabs
procession of lumbering clouds

border the altar   my bones in rare formation
I remember stumbling
through these steps before   cool-breeze naked
early wind   winged

callusing
coiling toes   bone now
worn and barrel
rolling   under an aguacero

downpour   soil over-
flowing from my toenails
river sloshing
in prayer   pruning

summoned storm
I have wept to life   once
I wore ruby feathers and
preferred the sky   now   I am

bended knees   blink flood
I see beyond this place   where clouds
gather   bend me rain
and maybe   I'll go away

COMMUNITY FARMING

this plot of farmland
in the middle of the city
wants green that can grow
anywhere   to be left
all over the kitchen   island
in a protest at Grand Central
a tattoo in a story   black fence of vines
with clean hands
falling into earth
like we all must
with slices of guava and queso
under tongue
you dropped this idea that
not too deep under this topsoil
was our ancestors
and we could hide
from our familiar in a marathon of digging
our dirty gospel book club
we recited the sun in apricot   Them   the shy pond
the pump   channeling a laughing candle
the power-walks to the train station
blurring the edges   of fence
and the air here makes me break out
a jade mattress   a prying spade
a green house on the corner
of cinder and brownstone
and the garden screened a film
for us to watch   for free   starring
Two in the Morning and *Pollo Guisado*
today   I joined the blur
heard the plants whisper about a silo
and attachment styles   con chili peppers
a long strand of hair
in my laundry   a seed

EULOGY FOR A MANGO TREE

i'm still the boy in the navy shorts running around
you with my shirt wrapped around my head
lifting a fallen branch   now   a leafed sword   you whisper
a breeze i could barely hear and i nod as if i understand

did you think less of me when home was a spiraled gust
and i returned to the thunder of my birth   fist rushing into wall   hiding
violently   some secrets sound like boiling salt water   don't they   carved
my name into you with a parrots claw   you were there   i fell asleep outside

my door on cobble road   did you whisper our stories to the horses in summer
on the darkest nights   where i'd stumble home a puddle of myself   why didn't
you just drink me   god lift you   wake me up with sweet prayers
as if to not embarrass me   who else do you offer refuge in your shadows

what other faces have you saved   you understood that the stars don't need
to see everything   when the sky arrived masked as a bursting mango
i'd share a cafecito with you   scoff in your bark   you'd admit you thought
you'd never see the day i'd like my coffee without cream

it's my secret to everlasting life   what's yours   tell me   tell me

NOTES

Sighting borrows language from Nas's "Nas Is Like."
Tonight's Blackout borrows language from Kanye West's "Gorgeous."
Left The Hotel FEMA Stopped Paying For On Friday borrows language from Nina Simone's "Baltimore."
Battered New is created entirely of newspaper headlines.
Catch A Glow is divided by lyrics from Hector Lavoe's "Periodico De Ayer."

Additional Acknowledgments

Thank you God.

Thank you Christen Kincaid and Finishing Line Press.

Thank you Mayda Del Valle, José Olivarez, and Willie Perdomo for your words and voices.

Thank you Vanessa Gabb and Cydney Edwards for your incredible care of many of these poems in their early stages.

Thank you to First Wave, Urban Word NYC, The Public Theater, and Hunts Point Alliance For Children for providing a space to explore verse. Thank you to all my students, past, present, future.

Thank you to Eric Mata, Josh Healy, Dasha Kelly for introducing me to the craft you loved so dearly.

Thank you Chris Walker and Rafael Casal for guiding me through stage, sound, and story.

Thank you to my Do or Die brothers.

Thank you to my chosen family: Sofía Snow, Kellen Abston, Danez Smith, Thiahera Nurse, Lorena Barbosa, Blaire White, Nat Iosbaker, James Gavins, Maurice Turner, Joshua Sarnowski, Quincy Jack, Malkia and Chike Stampley, Bianca Medina.

Thank you to my titís and tíos, sisters and cousins, nephews and nieces, my father for enabling me to tell our stories.

And thank you to my mother for your constant support and for taking me with you on your visits home to Puerto Rico.

Karl **Michael Iglesias** is an actor, director, and writer originally from Milwaukee, WI. A graduate of the University of Wisconsin and First Wave Hip Hop Theater Ensemble, he continues his exploration of verse and heightened language in theater. His poetry can be found in *Apogee*, *The Acentos Review*, *The Breakwater Review*, *The Florida Review*, *RHINO Poetry*, *Kweli Journal*, *Breakbeat Poets Vol. 4: LatiNext* (Haymarket Books, 2020), and *The Westchester Review*. Karl now resides in Brooklyn, New York.

Hip Hop.

CPSIA information can be obtained
at www.ICGtesting.com
Printed in the USA
BVHW031017240321
603275BV00007B/857